612
ARD

Ardley, Bridget

Skin, hair, and
teeth

DATE DUE			

HOW OUR BODIES WORK
SKIN, HAIR, AND TEETH
BRIDGET AND NEIL ARDLEY

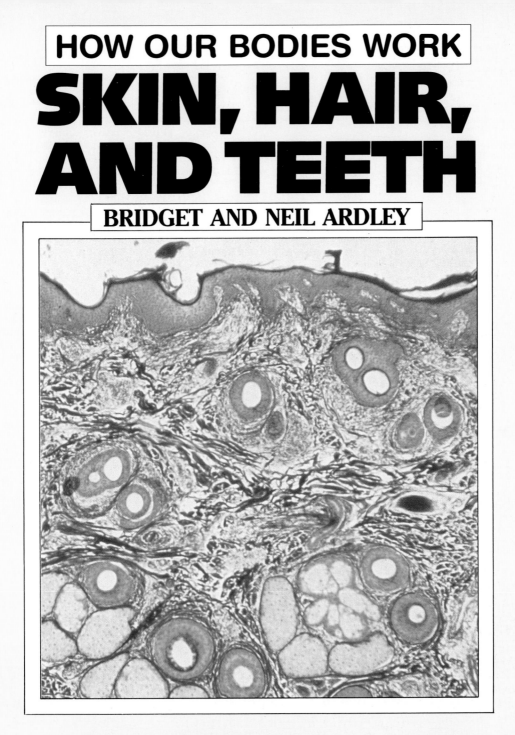

Editorial planning
Philip Steele

 SILVER BURDETT PRESS

Original copyright, © Macmillan Education Limited 1988
© BLA Publishing Limited 1988

Designed and produced by BLA Publishing Limited,
East Grinstead, Sussex, England.
A Ling Kee Company

Illustrations by David Cook/Linden Artists and Anna Hancock
Color origination by Waterden Reproductions
Printed in Hong Kong

88/89/90/91/92/93   6 5 4 3 2 1

Library of Congress Cataloging-in-Publication Data

Ardley, Neil.
    Skin, hair, and teeth/by Neil Ardley.
        p.   cm. — (How our bodies work)
    Includes index.
    Summary: Describes the functions, characteristics, disorders,
and care of skin, teeth, and hair.
    1. Skin — Juvenile literature. 2. Hair — Juvenile literature.
3. Teeth — Juvenile literature. [1. Skin. 2. Hair. 3. Teeth.]
I. Title. II. Series.
QP88.5.A73   1988
612'.79   dc 19   87-38112
                                                        CIP

ISBN 0-382-09706-8 (hardback)

Photographic credits

t = top b = bottom l = left r = right

cover: Trevor Hill

4 Camilla Jessell Photo Library; 5*t*, 5*b* Frank Lane
Picture Agency; 6*t* Bridgeman Art Library; 6*b* Ancient
Art and Architecture Collection; 7 Science Photo Library;
9*t*, 9*b* Trevor Hill; 10 Sporting Pictures; 11*t*, 11*b* Trevor
Hill; 12 Science Photo Library; 13*t*, 13*bl*, 13*br* Trevor
Hill; 14 Science Photo Library; 15*t* Trevor Hill; 15*b* Rex
Features; 16, 17*t* Trevor Hill; 17*b* J. Allan Cash;
18 St Bartholomew's Hospital; 18*b* Science Photo
Library; 19 S. & R. Greenhill; 20, 21, 22, 23*t* Trevor
Hill; 23 J. Allan Cash; 25 Trevor Hill; 26*t* J. Allan Cash;
26*b* Camilla Jessell Photo Library; 27, 28 Trevor Hill;
29*t*, 29*bl*, 29*br* Science Photo Library; 30, 31, 33*t*, 33*b*,
34, 35*t*, 35*b*, 36 Trevor Hill; 37*t* Science Photo Library;
37*b* Trevor Hill; 38 J. Allan Cash; 39*t* ZEFA;
39*b* S. & R. Greenhill; 40*t* Japanese Tourist Office;
40*b* J. Allan Cash; 41 Trevor Hill; 44 Science Photo
Library; 45*t* Mary Evans Picture Library; 45*b* Frank
Spooner Pictures

How To Use This Book:
This book has many useful features. For example, look at the table of contents. See how it describes
each section in the book. Find a section you want to read and turn to it.
    Notice that the section is a "two-page spread." That is, it covers two facing pages. Now look at
the headings in the spread. Headings are useful when you want to locate specific information. Next,
look at a photograph, drawing, chart or map and find its caption. Captions give you additional
information. A chart or map may also have labels to help you.
    Scan the spread for a word in **bold print**. If you cannot find one in this spread, find one in
another spread. Bold-print words are defined in the glossary at the end of the book. Find your
bold-print word in the glossary.
    Now turn to the index at the end of the book. When you have a specific topic or subject to
research, look for it in the index. you will quickly know whether the topic is in the book.
    We hope you will use the features in this book to help you learn about new and exciting things.

Contents

Introduction

▼ The way we look depends on our skin, hair, and teeth. Our skin forms a waterproof and heat-proof covering which protects the insides of our bodies.

What is the biggest organ in your body? You may be surprised to find out that it is the outer covering you call your skin. If you could take off your skin and stretch it out, it would cover an area the size of a large blanket.

Your skin is not only waterproof and elastic. It also protects your body. The hair on your head grows from your skin, as do the nails on your fingers and toes. The teeth in your mouth are rooted in the skin of the **gums**. You need to take good care of your skin, hair, and teeth, not only to look good, but to keep healthy.

Nonstop Action

Your skin helps your body work. Skin keeps blood inside your body. It also helps to keep the tiny **germs**, which make us sick, from getting inside the body. Your skin also keeps you cool if the weather is hot, and warm if it is cold. It works all the time to protect your body.

Your hair, nails, and teeth are not parts that keep your body working. You could live without them. However, you use your teeth to bite and chew food. Your hair helps to keep you warm. Your nails help to protect your fingers and toes from damage.

Body Design

People are not the only creatures to have skin, hair, nails, and teeth. Many animals have them, too. In fact, the reason that we have these parts of our bodies is because modern humans developed from very early humanlike creatures who had more of a need for them. These creatures lived long ago. Over millions of years, many of them were born and died. During this time, they changed in shape. Their bodies slowly **evolved** until they became the humans we are today.

Although many animals have skin, hair, nails, and teeth, they are used in many different ways. A frog, for example, can drink and breathe with its skin. The frog takes in water and air through tiny channels in the skin. Moles use their nails, or claws, to dig. Some snakes have needle-sharp teeth that are filled with poison to kill other animals when they bite them.

▲ This baby chimpanzee is covered with dark hair. Humans have little hair on their bodies. The skin, nails, and teeth of the chimpanzee are much like those of a human being.

► Frogs take in some of the air they need for breathing through their moist, green skins. The color of this tree frog makes it hard to see among the leaves. This helps it hide from its enemies.

5

Finding Out

▼ The Bible tells the story of Samson, who was a man of great strength. The secret of Samson's strength was in his hair. Samson loved Delilah, but she betrayed him. A man cut off Samson's hair while he was sleeping. Samson lost all his strength and was captured by his enemies.

Early people knew very little about how the body works. They could not do much to help themselves if something went wrong with their skin, hair, or teeth. They also had ideas about their bodies which we now know are wrong.

Magic Powers

In ancient times, people thought that parts of the body contained magic. They believed that if they could get some hair from a person, or even some nail clippings, then they would have power over the person. They thought they owned part of that person's body.

Hair was thought to have great power. The rulers of ancient Egypt, called Pharaohs, wore wigs of gold or silver on their heads. The Pharaohs, male and female, also attached long false beards to their chins because beards were a sign of power.

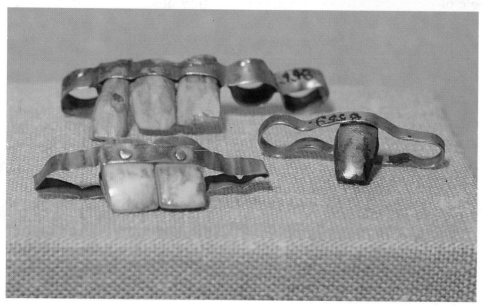

◄ False teeth were made by the Etruscans, in Italy, over 2,500 years ago. Gold bridges were used to hold human teeth, ox teeth, or false teeth made of ivory.

▲ The use of microscopes helped scientists understand how the skin is formed. This photograph, taken with a very powerful microscope, shows the surface of the skin and a shaft of body hair.

The First Doctors

Although the people of long ago did not know how to cure serious illnesses, they could deal with small problems. The peoples of ancient Egypt even knew how to make a kind of bandage to cover wounds on the skin. They also made **ointments** and medicines from plants. The ointments helped to clear itchy patches, or **rashes**, on the skin. However, some diseases left marks on the skin that nothing could remove.

A toothache was a terrible problem. Medicines made from plants helped to reduce the pain. However, early people usually pulled out teeth that hurt or rotted. False teeth made of materials like ivory, wood, gold and silver, or from animal or human teeth were used to replace the missing teeth.

The Age of Science

Over the past 400 years, people have found out a lot about the body and how it works. Scientists have made many important discoveries about the body. They often use **microscopes**, so that they can see very tiny objects or parts of things more clearly.

The first scientist to use a microscope to look at skin was Anton van Leeuwenhoek, who lived in the Netherlands. In the 1600s, he found out that skin has several layers. Leeuwenhoek also looked at hair through his microscope. He saw that hair is made of layers, too.

Scientists also discovered that all living things are made of billions of tiny units called **cells**. Scientists first saw cells in plants. In 1839, the German scientist, Theodor Schwann, found that animals are made of cells, too. This discovery helped to explain how skin, hair, and teeth grow. Knowing this, doctors have been able to find good ways to treat them.

What Is Skin?

▼ If you could look inside your skin, you would see that it is made up of two layers. In the bottom layer are the roots of your hair and tiny blood vessels. There are glands which make sweat and glands which produce oil. There are also the endings of nerves.

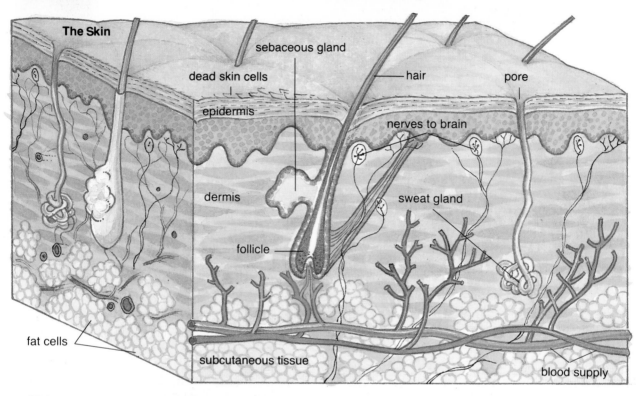

The Skin

sebaceous gland

dead skin cells

epidermis

hair

pore

nerves to brain

dermis

sweat gland

follicle

fat cells

subcutaneous tissue

blood supply

Skin covers the whole of the surface of the body and also the inside of the mouth and nose. Your skin would cover an area of ten square feet if it could be stretched out flat. Now, your whole skin weighs about six and a half pounds. As you grow older, it will get heavier.

Your skin does not have the same thickness all over your body. Your eyelids have the thinnest skin. They are only ¹⁄₅₀ of an inch thick. The thickest skin on your body is found on the soles of your feet. It is ¼ of an inch thick.

Skin is made of cells that are too small to be seen. Millions of them are packed together in your skin, which has several layers. The top layer is the **epidermis**. On the outside are dead cells, which rub off all the time. New cells are always forming inside your skin. The cells live for about three weeks, and move toward the outside of the skin where they die, and flake off.

Under Your Skin

There are short hairs growing out from most of your skin. The roots of these hairs are in channels called **follicles**.

When you get hot, you lose water from your body. The water passes through the skin as **sweat**. This helps to cool your body, although it can be harmful if you lose too much water. In your skin, there are lots of tiny holes called **pores**. These pores are the tops of narrow channels that lead down to millions of tiny **glands** that produce the sweat.

▲ A child has smooth skin. This is because the skin is very elastic in the young. It moves back into place easily when it is stretched.

The hair follicles and sweat glands are in the **dermis**. This is the layer of skin under the epidermis. This layer also contains other glands called **sebaceous glands**, which make a kind of oil. This oil covers and protects your skin and hair.

In the dermis, there are also many narrow tubes through which blood flows. These blood vessels carry the blood from your heart, which pumps about one third of all your blood to the skin. There are long thin fibers that also run through the dermis and epidermis. These are **nerves** that go from the skin to the brain. The nerves make the skin able to feel things.

Underneath the dermis is another layer called the **subcutaneous tissue**. This layer is not part of the skin. It is made of fat, and it helps to keep your body warm.

▲ An elderly person's skin has more folds and wrinkles, especially on the face and hands. The skin is less elastic in old age, and fits the body less tightly.

What Skin Does

Your skin protects your body. The oil, or **sebum**, from the sebaceous glands makes the skin waterproof. It stops water from entering the flesh beneath the skin. Also, the sebum helps to kill germs on the skin. Unless the skin is cut or broken, very few germs can get through it into the body. The skin has other important uses, too.

Hot and Cold

Humans are warm-blooded animals. This means that inside your body, the **temperature** is normally always the same. It does not get hotter or colder unless you are sick. Your skin helps to control your temperature. If your skin is hot, or if you get hot by running or working hard, the blood vessels near the surface widen. More blood flows close to the surface. Heat passes from the warm blood through the skin and helps you to lose the extra heat. You produce more sweat from your pores, too. The water in the sweat passes into the air by **evaporation** . This makes your skin cooler.

If it is cold, the blood vessels narrow, so that less blood flows near the surface. More heat stays in your body and helps you to stay warm. Tiny **muscles** around the hairs on your skin pull together to make the hairs stand up. The muscles make the little lumps we call goose pimples. The raised hairs trap air around your body. This layer of air stops heat from leaving your skin.

Getting Rid of Waste

When you eat food and take a drink, your body makes waste products from them. Some of these wastes enter the blood, which carries them to the skin. From the blood, the wastes go into the sweat glands. When you sweat, you lose these waste products. The wastes include salt, so sometimes your skin gets slightly salty. Every day your skin makes more than a pint of sweat.

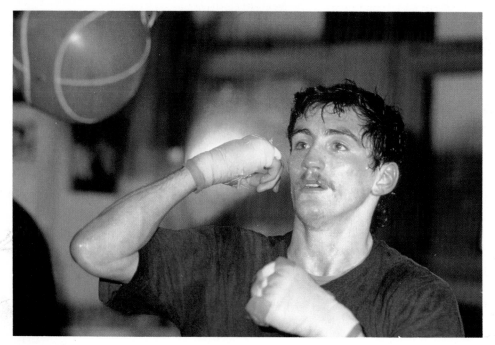

◄ The British boxer, Barry McGuigan, is practicing with a punching ball. It is hot work. He is sweating and has become red in the face. The redness is caused by blood rushing to the skin. The extra blood and the sweating help to cool the body.

Messages to the Brain

When you touch an object, you can feel it. You can also tell whether it is hot or cold. This is because the nerves in your skin send messages to the brain. The messages are electrical signals. As the brain gets the signals, you feel the object.

Feeling is one of the most important ways in which the skin helps the body. It warns you of very hot or very cold objects, so that you do not touch them and damage the skin. You also feel pain if your skin is touched by any object that may damage it. This tells you that you are in danger. The messages to the brain make you move away from the object very quickly.

▲ When you stroke a cat, you can feel that its fur is soft. The nerves in your fingers send messages about the texture to the brain.

▼ The brain gets pain messages from the skin when you graze, cut, or burn yourself. The messages tell you that you are hurt and that you need help.

Skin Color

▼ This is a photograph of some skin, taken with a microscope. The dark spots are the layer of melanin in the skin.

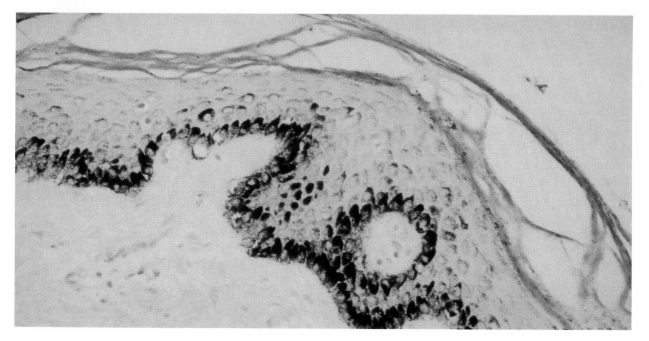

People throughout the world have skins of different colors. Some are very, very dark and others are light brown. Some people's skin has a yellowish tint. Other people have very light skin. In people with very, very pale skin, the blood under the skin can show through. This makes them look pink or even red, especially if they are hot. In most people the color is in the top layer of the skin. We get this color from our ancestors.

Skin color is still another way in which the skin helps the body. Invisible rays called **ultraviolet rays** reach us from the sun. These rays can harm the body if we are out in a lot of sunshine. Therefore, the epidermis contains a dark-colored **pigment**. This pigment is called **melanin**. The melanin absorbs the ultraviolet rays, so that they do not pass through the skin and into the body.

As humans evolved, the people who lived in hot places had dark skins with lots of melanin to protect them from the sun. In cooler parts of the world, people needed less protection from the sun. In cold places with little sunshine, people had pale skins without much pigment. In some parts of the world there is also a pigment called **carotene** which is found in the dermis. The people whose ancestors came from those places have more carotene in their skin than other people. The carotene gives their skin a faint yellowish tint.

Over the centuries, people have moved to live in different parts of the world. However, all of us still have the same skin color as our parents or grandparents. Sometimes, two people with different colored skin will have children. These children may have darker or lighter skin than one of their parents.

▲ This boy's skin is dark brown. It contains a lot of the dark pigment called melanin.

Getting a Suntan

People with pale skins will turn a darker color if they are often in the sun. The skin produces extra melanin to protect the body against the extra ultraviolet rays. Their skin will turn browner within a few days. The suntan fades gradually when there is less sunshine.

Patchy or Pale

Many people have freckles. These are dark, brownish spots of color in the skin. Freckles are parts of the skin which have more melanin. Moles, like freckles, are parts of the skin that have more pigment. However, they normally appear on their own rather than in clusters. Often, moles are raised and slightly hairy.

A few people have no pigment at all. They have very pale skins and white hair. These people are called **albinos**. Their skin is unable to make any pigment because of a defect in their **genes**. Albinos have to be very careful in the sun.

▲ This Chinese boy has yellowish skin. Many East Asian people have a pigment called carotene in their skin.

▲ This girl has a pale skin with little pigment in it. However, there is more pigment in her brown freckles.

New Skin
for Old

Your skin is alive just like the rest of your body. Under the surface, it is made of living cells packed together. As they live, the cells split apart, forming new skin cells all the time.

The cells move to the surface of the skin slowly. There, they die and form the tough surface of the skin. Tiny white scales of dead cells fall off the skin. Then, more cells come up from below to replace them.

Cuts and Wounds

New skin is forming all the time, so that your skin can repair itself. If you get a small cut or graze, it soon heals and normally leaves no mark. Skin cells move into the gap made by the cut or graze and fill it with new skin.

If you get a wound, it is important to treat it. Harmful germs can easily enter any gap in the skin. Washing the wound removes dirt that contains germs. Using an **antiseptic** kills the germs. Placing a clean bandage over the wound helps to keep more germs from getting in.

A cut or graze usually bleeds for a short time. Then, the flow of blood stops. Inside the blood, tangles of small strands of cells called **fibrin** form. The fibrin traps cells in the blood, and makes the blood sticky. Then, the blood dries, and a hard scab forms over the wound. The scab keeps germs from getting in while new skin grows underneath. When the new skin is in place the scab falls off.

▼ **This magnified picture shows a network of fibrin forming in the blood. It is trapping red blood cells, which here have been colored yellow so that they are easier to see. This is how blood thickens and forms a scab when you cut yourself.**

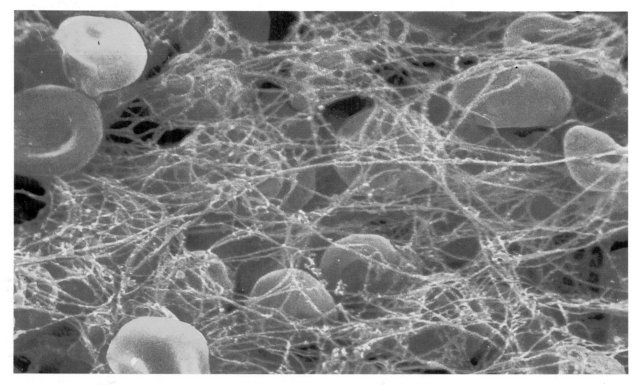

Replacing Skin

If a cut or graze only breaks the epidermis, then it will leave no mark when it heals. However, if the wound goes into the dermis, a **scar** may form as the skin heals. Fibers from the dermis enter the new skin as it heals, and the skin becomes hard. The scar makes a mark on the skin that may not go away.

If a person has a bad skin wound, such as a large burn, scars may form that look very ugly. Doctors can do a **skin graft** to keep a scar from forming. They cut a thin layer of skin from another part of the person's body, such as a leg or the back. Then, they place the layer of skin on the wound. This skin begins to grow over the wound. The wound heals quickly without scars. New skin grows in a normal way on the part of the body from which the graft was taken.

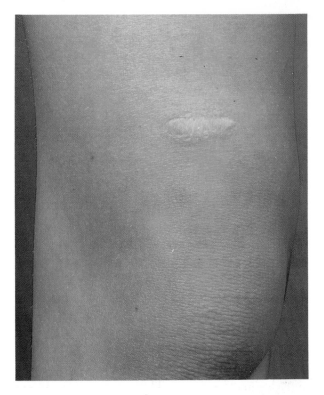

▲ The mark on this leg is a scar which has formed after a bad injury. Because the wound was deep, the skin did not grow back in the same way. A small scar may slowly disappear, but this may take a long time.

◄ Fire engines and ambulances rush to the scene of a fire. Doctors today can save many victims of fires. They can treat very bad burns, and graft on new skin to replace the old.

Taking Care of the Skin

Your skin is very important to your body. You should take care of it and keep it healthy. Damaged skin makes it easy for germs to get into your body. Dirty skin will let germs grow.

Pimples

There are substances in the blood which make changes happen in the body. These **hormones** can reach every cell in the body and are important because they make the body work properly. As you start to grow up, hormones cause changes in your skin. The sebaceous glands get bigger and produce more oily sebum. This may block pores and the plugs of sebum may appear as **blackheads**. If the blackheads are not washed away, germs may grow in them. These germs can spread and cause pimples called **acne**. However, if the sebaceous glands do not produce enough sebum, the skin may become dry, flaky, and sore.

Keeping clean is important. You need to wash regularly to keep your skin free of oil, dirt, germs, and dead skin cells.

Eating a wide variety of food will also help you to have clear and healthy skin. Especially, you should eat plenty of vegetables and fruit to keep your skin in good condition. It is also important to drink a lot of water.

▼ A healthy diet is one which includes a variety of fresh foods. Fruit, vegetables, and dairy products help to keep your skin clear and healthy.

► When you go to the bathroom, you should always wash your hands afterwards. Always wash them before you eat. Your skin may have picked up germs which could make you sick if swallowed with your food.

▼ If you lie out in the sun, your skin becomes suntanned. Screening creams or lotions can be used to protect the skin from harmful rays in the sunshine. Too much sunbathing can be bad for you.

Protecting the Skin

Many people lie in the sun because they think tanned skin makes them look nicer. However, too much sun can be harmful. Light-colored skin, which does not have much melanin to protect it from the sun's ultraviolet rays, can get badly sunburned. The skin gets red and sore, and little bubbles of fluid, or **blisters**, may form. Ultraviolet rays may also damage the fibers in the skin that make it soft and elastic.

Regular sunbathing may make skin dry, rough, and wrinkly. Also, doctors believe that too much sun can cause changes in skin cells which may result in skin **cancer**. Cancer is most likely to develop on those areas of the skin that get the most sun.

If you do want to lie in the sun, you should always protect your skin with special lotions or creams that will block the ultraviolet rays. There are also creams to protect the skin from strong winds and very cold weather.

Skin Problems

Several things can go wrong with your skin. Teenagers often suffer from acne because their skin gets oily and the oil traps germs. Washing regularly will help to get rid of the oil. Special antiseptic creams that kill germs will also help. If acne is bad, it is a good idea to go to a doctor. The doctor will be able to give advice and medicine which will help to clear it up.

Sometimes, large painful swelling on the skin is caused by germs. This is a **boil**. The skin around a boil must be kept very clean. The boil should be allowed to burst naturally. If a boil is very big and painful, a doctor will open it and clean it out with an antiseptic. A group of boils is called a carbuncle.

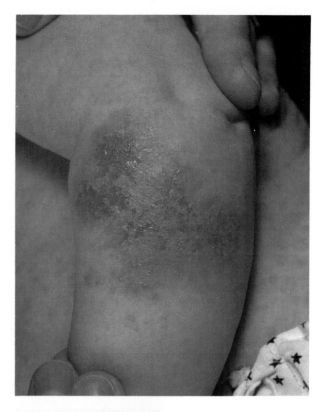

▲ Eczema can be very painful and itchy. The skin on this child's arm has become blistered and sore.

◄ A microscope shows a head louse clinging to human hair. Lice are parasites which suck blood from the skin. They can cause itching and skin infections.

Itchy Skin

Damaged cells can make your skin red and hot. It is often itchy, too. A rash may appear on the surface of the skin. **Dermatitis** is an itchy red rash. **Eczema** is a similar kind of rash which is often flaky, as well as being very itchy. Both of these rashes may be caused by an **allergy**. This happens when you have touched or eaten something that your body does not like.

People may be allergic to wool, to plants, to dust in the air, or to some of the things that they eat.

Itching can also be caused by **parasites**. These are tiny creatures that live on the body or in clothes. Two of the most common parasites are lice and fleas, which suck blood.

▼ This baby has a bad attack of chicken pox. His skin is covered with itchy spots. His brother has already had the disease, so he will not catch it again.

Feeling Sick

People can catch some illnesses from each other. These are known as **infectious diseases**. Some infectious diseases may show on the skin. Measles shows as a blotchy red rash which starts on the face and spreads over the body. Chicken pox causes spots which become blisters and scabs. The marks on your skin will help the doctor tell what is wrong with you.

When you have an infectious disease, your skin may feel very hot. This is a sign that your body is trying to fight off the disease. More blood goes to the skin. The blood is carrying **white blood cells** which are the body's defenders. The white blood cells destroy the bacteria and clear away any waste. While they are doing this, they make a lot of heat, and you need to cool off through your skin. Good health care and hygiene can help to prevent the spread of infectious diseases.

Our Nails

Each of your nails grows out of a deep fold in the skin of your fingers and toes. Nails are made of a hard material that is made by special cells in the epidermis. This material is called **keratin**. Keratin also forms a tough layer on the surface of the skin. As cells move up to the surface of the skin, they become packed with keratin. As they die, the thin layer of keratin forms. Nails are a very thick layer of solid keratin.

The skin beneath the nail covers the **quick**, which is the living root of the nail. The part of the nail you can see, the keratin plate, grows out of the quick. The plate moves forward as the cells change into keratin. This makes your nails grow. They grow about ⅛ of an inch each month.

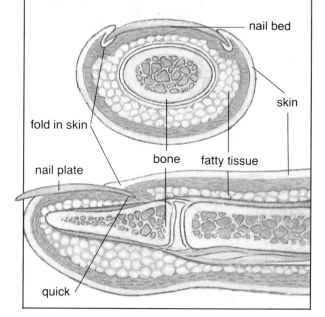

This is the inside of a finger. The finger bone is in the center, with fatty tissue around it. Skin lies on top of the tissue, and the nail plate grows from a deep fold in the skin. A toenail grows in the same way.

nail bed

skin

fold in skin

bone   fatty tissue

nail plate

quick

◀ Nails protect the ends of the fingers. They are made of keratin, a hard material which does not break easily. Fingernails help the tips of the fingers to grip objects firmly, so that we can lift and carry them.

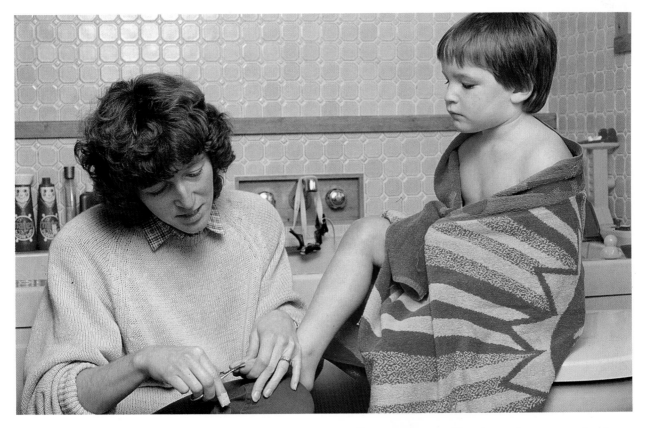

▲ It is important to take care of our nails by trimming them and keeping them clean. A broken or injured nail can be very painful.

The ends of our fingers can feel even very tiny objects. They are very **sensitive** because there are over 48,000 nerve endings in each square inch. The nails are tough to help protect the ends of our fingers and toes from damage or pain. Fingernails also make the ends of our fingers firm so that we can pick up and hold things. Their sharp edges also allow us to do some difficult things like untying knotted shoelaces.

Nail Care

You should take good care of your nails. If you do not, they could look ugly, get in the way, or break painfully. The best way to keep your nails clean is to scrub them with a nailbrush every time you wash your hands. This will get rid of any dirt and germs trapped under the nails. Gently push back the skin at the bottom of your nails when you dry them. Do this very carefully or you may damage the quick.

You can cut or file your nails without hurting yourself because they are made of dead keratin. Your fingernails should be rounded. Sharp corners might catch on things, and cause your nails to tear. This can damage the quick.

Your toenails should be cut straight across. If they are not, the nail may grow into the skin of the toe. Ingrown toenails are very painful. Biting your fingernails may cause them to grow in as well. Damage caused by biting nails can lead to infection of the quick. It can also help the germs under your fingernails to get into your body.

Why Do We Have Hair?

Many warm-blooded creatures are covered with hair or fur. This is used to help them control their body temperature. We have hair because we evolved from animals with hair. Early people were much hairier than we are now. They needed this hair to keep them warm. Much of the hair stopped growing as people evolved. People can now live without a lot of hair because they can make clothes to keep themselves warm in colder weather.

▼ This baby has only a little hair on his head. Soon he will grow a full head of hair. Your hair helps to keep you warm, because it stops some heat from leaving your body.

All of our skin is still covered with some hair except for the palms of our hands, soles of our feet, and lips and mouth. However, most of our hair now grows on our heads.

We have kept the hair on our heads because we lose a lot of our body heat through our heads. People in a cold climate need to put extra cover on their heads. People can survive without hair. Young babies have very little hair and many men lose their hair as they grow older. They may need to cover their heads more often than other people. However, they do not become sick because of the lack of hair.

Growing Up

Some babies have a full head of hair when they are born. Often, this hair soon drops out. There is nothing wrong with the baby. It simply begins to grow new hair. This may be of a different color from the

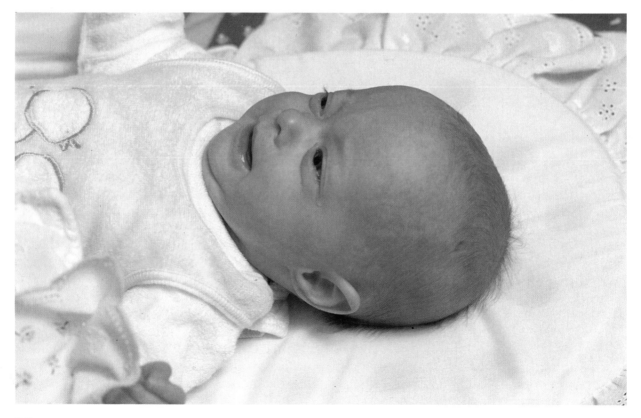

hair it had at birth. By their third birthdays, most children have a good head of hair. It does not change much as they grow up, although blond hair often gets darker.

Children also have very fine hairs that you can hardly see on most of the rest of their skin. They grow more body hair at **puberty**, which is the age when children begin to change into adults. Thicker hair grows on the arms and legs, in the armpits, and in the pubic region between the legs. As boys become men, they grow hairs on the face. Many shave this hair off because they do not want a beard or mustache. Men may also grow hair on the chest and back.

These changes in our bodies are caused by hormones. They cause the hair follicles to grow hair and the sebaceous glands to start working. Some hormones can also stop hair from growing. This is why many men go bald. Women do not go bald because they have different hormones.

▲ This man has lost most of the hair on his head. He is bald because the hormones in his body have caused his hair to stop growing. This kind of baldness is very common and is not harmful.

▶ Bearded Sikhs guard the Golden Temple in Amritsar, India. Male Sikhs wear beards as part of their religion. Many men like to wear beards because they think it looks attractive. Other men prefer to shave.

How Hair Grows

You have about 100,000 hairs on your head. The hair grows out of the skin on your head, or **scalp**. Each hair is very strong, even though it is so thin. This is because hair, like your nails, is made of tough keratin.

Rooted in Skin

Each hair has its root in a hair follicle in the dermis of the skin. At the base of each follicle, cells containing keratin pack together to form the root of the hair. As new cells with keratin form, the hair grows up from the root and out of the follicle. The cells die as the hair reaches the surface of the skin. The hair becomes a dead **shaft** of keratin.

As each hair grows, a sebaceous gland at the root coats it with a little oil. This keeps the hair in good condition, and may make it look shiny.

Each hair grows about ¼ of an inch every month. It keeps on growing for as long as six years. Then, the hair falls out and another hair starts to grow in its place. You lose about one hundred hairs every day. This loss does not show because you have so many other hairs on your head.

Curly or Straight?

People have different kinds of hair. It may be thick and coarse or thin and fluffy. You may have hair that is naturally curly, wavy, or straight.

The kind of hair that you have depends on the size and shape of each follicle. If the follicle is large, the hair shaft will be thick. Narrow follicles produce thin hair. The shape of the follicle can make the shaft bend so that the hair has curls or waves.

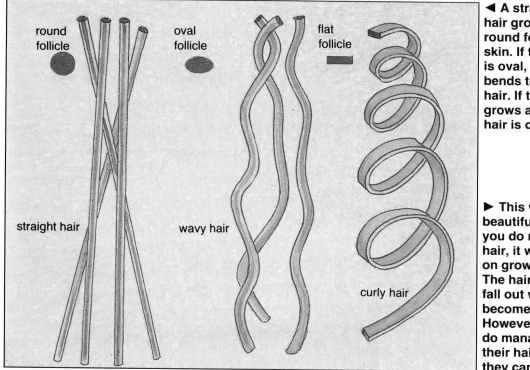

round follicle

oval follicle

flat follicle

straight hair

wavy hair

curly hair

◀ **A straight shaft of hair grows from a round follicle in the skin. If the hair follicle is oval, the shaft bends to give wavy hair. If the follicle grows a flat shaft, the hair is curly.**

▶ **This woman has beautiful, long hair. If you do not cut your hair, it will not keep on growing for ever. The hairs will tend to fall out when they become very long. However, some people do manage to grow their hair so long that they can sit on it!**

Hair Color

Along with being coarse, fine, straight, waved, or curly, your hair also has a certain color. It can be black, brown, red, or blond, or even any shade among these colors.

You are born with hair of a certain color. It is usually like that of your parents or grandparents. The kind of hair you have also comes from your ancestors. If they came from Africa, your hair is likely to be black and curly. People from Asia often have straight black hair. In northern Europe, many people have blond or red hair that is straight or wavy.

▲ This West Indian girl has black, curly hair. The hair contains melanin, the pigment which also makes her skin dark. She has braided her hair tightly.

◄ This brother and sister have red, wavy hair. We normally have the same kind and color of hair as our parents.

Natural Colors

Your hair has a certain natural color for the same reason that your skin is a certain color. It contains pigment. Your skin feeds the pigment to your hair as it grows.

Each hair on your head has three parts. At the center is the **medulla**, which is soft. Around it is the **cortex**, which is the main part of the hair. The outer layer is the **cuticle**. It is hard and protects the hair shaft.

The cortex makes the hair tough and elastic. It also contains the pigments that give the hair its color. The color of your hair depends on which pigments you have and how much of each pigment is in the hair. Hair pigments are black, red, and yellow. Mixtures of the pigments give all kinds of hair colors.

When we get older, the skin stops feeding pigment to the hair and it turns gray or white. Albinos have white hair because their skin does not make pigment. Some people have a patch of white hair which does not get any pigment.

Changing Color

Many people color their hair. They use dyes to do this. Often, they dye their hair just to look different. People with gray or white hair may color it because they think darker hair makes them look younger. The hair must be colored often. This is because the natural color soon shows at the roots as the hair grows.

▼ As people become older, their hair turns white. The body no longer produces pigment to color the hair.

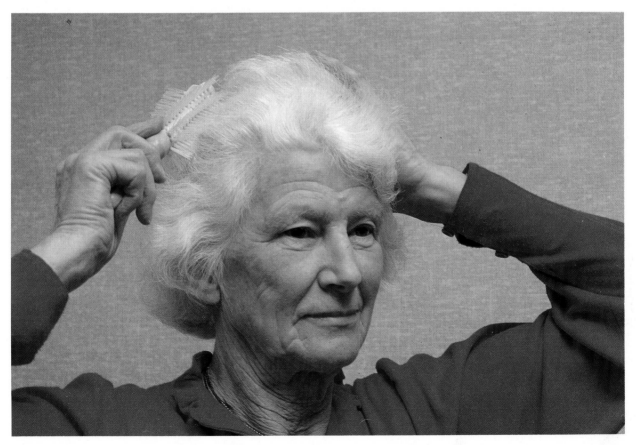

Hair Care

Sometimes people have problems with their hair. One of the most common is **dandruff**. This is dead skin that flakes off the scalp. It can be caused by the sebaceous glands making too little or too much sebum. If people are sick their hair often loses its shine and gets out of condition. This problem usually goes away when people get better.

Sometimes, parasites become hair problems. **Head lice** are common among young children. The lice lay eggs called nits which stick to the hairs. The lice can be removed with a special shampoo.

Ringworm is caused by an infection. It is not caused by a worm. Round scaly patches form on the body and scalp. Sometimes, the hairs break off, and leave little bald patches. Ringworm is spread by scratching. It should be treated by a doctor.

Sometimes, people lose their hair for other reasons. **Alopecia** is a condition where the hair falls out in patches. There is usually no obvious reason for this, and the hair often starts to grow again without treatment. People being treated with certain drugs may lose their hair. It usually grows back when the treatment stops. It has even been known for people to lose their hair if they have a bad shock.

Clean Hair

Although many hair problems are not caused because hair is dirty, it is very important to keep your hair in good condition. It should be washed regularly, especially if you live in a city.

You should avoid harsh shampoos because they could dry out the natural oil made by your scalp. It is not a good idea to rub your hair or scalp too hard, and you

◄ Washing your hair regularly will help to keep it free of parasites and dandruff. Do not wash it too often with strong shampoo, or you might dry out your scalp.

should make sure that your hair is rinsed thoroughly. If possible, your hair should be allowed to dry naturally. If you use a hair dryer, do not use the hot setting because heat can damage your hair.

Sometimes, the ends of your hair may split. This may be caused by rough treatment or by using a dryer that is too hot. Split ends can never be fixed. They can only be cut off.

Comb and brush your hair gently. If you tug at it, you can damage it. Brush your hair only when it is dry because wet hair breaks more easily. Keep your brush and comb clean, and never share them with other people. Sharing brushes, combs, barrettes, or hats can spread disease or parasites.

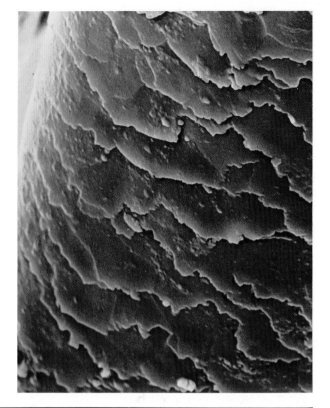

► This picture shows a shaft of hair magnified 500 times. You can see how the scales of keratin overlap each other.

The shafts of healthy hair are smooth and unbroken.

Split ends, such as the one shown, will not mend. They need to be cut off.

Our Teeth

Teeth are very important to our health. Without strong teeth, we would not be able to chew food. Healthy teeth look nice, too. Like your skin and hair, you must take care of your teeth by cleaning them. You should visit the dentist, so that your teeth can be checked to keep them healthy.

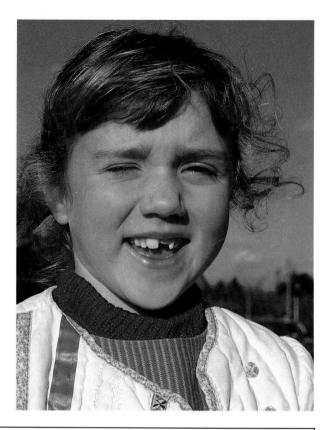

▶ This girl has a gap in her teeth because a milk tooth has fallen out. A new tooth will soon grow to replace the missing tooth.

▼ This is how one of your teeth would look if it were cut in half. On the outside is the hard enamel, which makes teeth strong and protects them from germs. The root fixes the tooth firmly into the jawbone in your mouth.

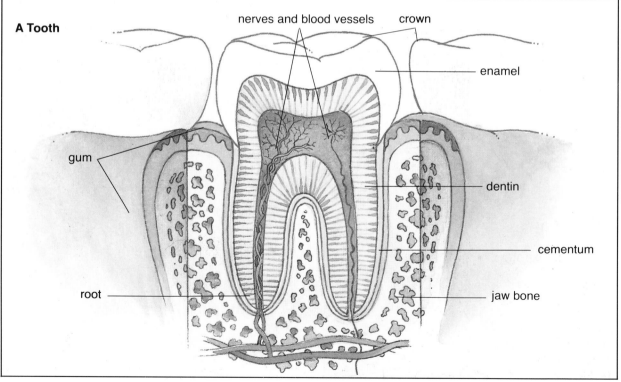

A Tooth

nerves and blood vessels   crown

enamel

gum

dentin

cementum

root

jaw bone

Kinds of Teeth

You did not have any teeth when you were born. Newborn babies only drink milk, so they do not need to have teeth.

During their lives, people will have two sets of teeth. The first teeth are called the **milk teeth**. They form by the time a child is two years old. There are twenty milk teeth. They begin to fall out at about the age of five or six.

The second set of teeth forms in place of the milk teeth. These are the teeth you keep all your life. There are thirty-two of these teeth, and usually they have all come through by the age of twenty-one.

You have several different kinds of teeth. At the front are **incisors**. These are sharp, square teeth that bite the food. At each side of the incisors are the **canines**. They are pointed teeth which help to tear food. Next, are the **premolars**, which crush the food. At the back are the **molars**. They are broad teeth that grind food.

What Are Teeth Made Of?

You can only see a part of the teeth in your mouth. Each tooth fits into a hole in the jawbone. Then, the lower part of the tooth is held firmly in place by the gums. The gums are part of the dermis which lines the mouth and covers the jawbone.

The hidden part of each tooth is its root. The white part that you can see is called the **crown** of the tooth. The crown is covered and protected by hard **enamel**, which is the hardest substance in your body. The enamel helps teeth to be very tough.

Under the enamel is a layer of yellow bone-like **dentin**. Dentin is softer than the enamel. Inside the dentin is the **pulp** of the tooth. The pulp is soft and it contains blood vessels and nerve fibers.

Both the dentin and pulp extend into the root. The outside of the root is covered by a bony layer of **cementum**, which holds the tooth in place.

▶ Without teeth, we would find it difficult to bite into hard foods, such as this stick of celery. Teeth also help us to speak, because the tongue strikes the teeth as we say certain words.

Taking Care of Our Teeth

Food left on your teeth attracts germs, just like dirty dishes that are not washed. A coating of millions of germs, called **plaque**, grows on the surface of your teeth. If you scrape a tooth gently with your nail, you will see the white film of plaque. Most plaque grows between the teeth and at the edges of the gums.

The germs in the plaque make **acid** as they feed on the bits of food in the mouth. More acid is made if the food is sugary. The acid attacks the enamel and starts to eat into the tooth, which causes tooth **decay**. If the decay goes through to the pulp, you will get a toothache. Plaque may also cause gum disease. To avoid tooth decay and gum disease, brush and floss your teeth often and visit the dentist regularly.

Daily Brushing

The way to remove plaque from your teeth is to brush them three times a day. Try to do this after each meal. At least, you should always brush them after breakfast and just before you go to bed. Your toothbrush should not be too hard.

Make sure the toothpaste you use has **fluoride** in it because this helps to reduce decay. Use a small quantity of toothpaste. Brush the top and bottom teeth separately. Move the brush up and down and in circles. It is important to brush every surface, especially along the gums.

Another important way to clean your teeth is with dental floss. Your dentist can show you how to use it correctly. Daily flossing is very important because it helps to get rid of plaque between your teeth, where your toothbrush cannot reach.

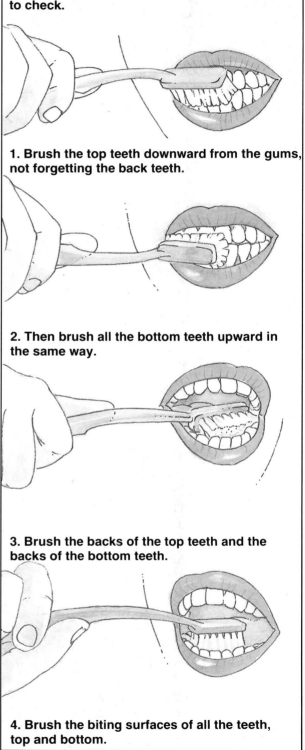

Brush your teeth for three minutes every time you clean them. You could use an egg-timer to check.

1. Brush the top teeth downward from the gums, not forgetting the back teeth.

2. Then brush all the bottom teeth upward in the same way.

3. Brush the backs of the top teeth and the backs of the bottom teeth.

4. Brush the biting surfaces of all the teeth, top and bottom.

No Sugar

Foods and drinks containing sweet-tasting sugar are very bad for your teeth. It is better to eat fruit and nuts for snacks and to drink sugar-free drinks. Milk, cheese, and green vegetables contain **calcium** which helps keep your bones and teeth hard. These foods also contain other **minerals** that are good for the teeth. Chewing hard food like apples helps. Dentists say that too much soft food can be bad for your teeth.

◄ It can be fun to use disclosing tablets or solutions. The dye they contain is harmless, and simply stains plaque red. This helps you to see the places you have missed when cleaning your teeth. Proper brushing will make the plaque disappear, so that you will not look like Dracula!

▼ If you try to avoid sugary foods like these, you should have less plaque and get fewer cavities. Try not to eat too much candy, chocolates, cookies, cakes, and jam. If you do eat sugary foods, brush your teeth afterwards.

Going to the Dentist

▼ This dentist is doing a regular check-up. The hygienist writes down details of the patient's teeth on a chart.

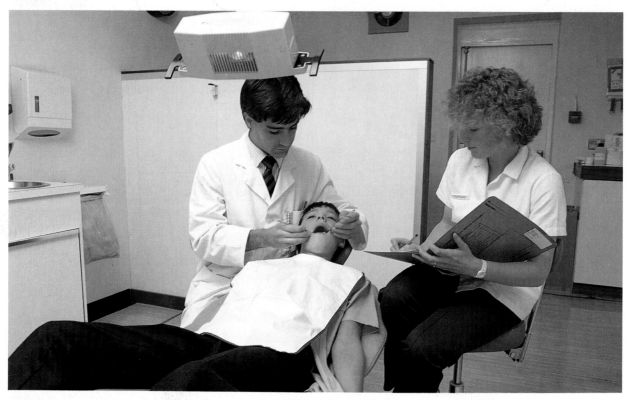

Some people do not go to the dentist often. Regular visits to the dentist can help to keep you from getting cavities. You should have a check-up every six months, so that the dentist can clean and examine your teeth. He or she looks at each tooth very carefully by using a little mirror. The dentist may also use a metal instrument called a **probe** to remove any bits of food stuck between your teeth.

The dental hygienist or assistant writes down all the details about your teeth. This helps the dentist to keep a record of how your teeth are growing. If you are lucky you may not have any cavities. Then, the dentist or hygienist just cleans and polishes your teeth.

Repairing the Teeth

No matter how carefully you take care of your teeth, you may sometimes develop decay that the dentist has to repair. First, you will be given an **injection** of a painkiller so that you will not feel any pain. This makes the area numb, so that you do not feel the dental instruments.

Then, the dentist uses a fine drill to cut away the decay in your tooth. He or she cleans out the hole with small tools called **excavators**. When the hole is ready, the dentist fills it with **amalgam**, which is a mixture of silver and other metals. Sometimes, adults have their teeth filled with gold or thin sheets of gold foil which will last a long time.

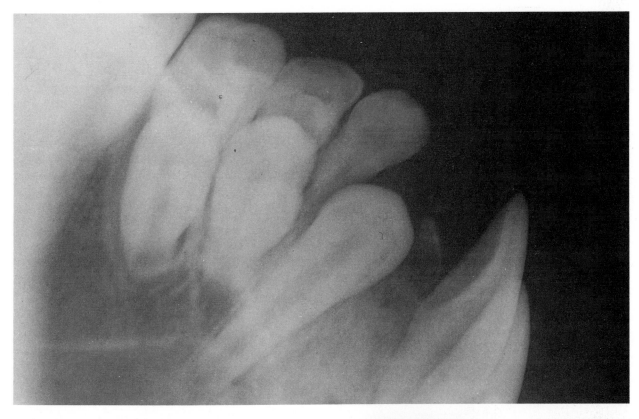

▲ Dentists use X-ray pictures to show up parts of the teeth and jawbone that they cannot see.

▶ A dentist needs special equipment in the surgery. Dental work must be carried out under bright lights. A small mirror may be used to look inside the patient's mouth.

A Dentist's Work

Sometimes, the dentist decides to take special photographs of your teeth, called **X-rays**. These show the inside of a tooth and whether there is any decay or damage. The dentist puts a small piece of film in your mouth before pointing the X-ray machine at your face. X-rays are only taken when they are necessary.

If a tooth is badly decayed or damaged, the dentist may decide to remove it. He or she will give the patient an **anesthetic** to keep the person from feeling pain. When the tooth has been pulled out, the gum may be a little sore. It will soon feel better.

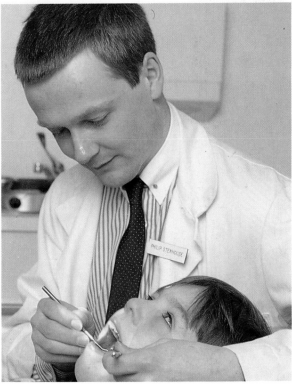

Dental Work

Sometimes, a dentist has to do more than simply fill or take out a tooth. If a tooth is badly damaged in an accident, a false crown may be needed to cover all or most of it. The dentist drills away the damaged enamel and takes an **impression**, or mould of the tooth. The crown is made by a person who is trained to make up false teeth. This is a dental technician. The dentist cements the crown into place. If a whole tooth is missing, a false one can be attached to healthy teeth on either side of the gap. This is called a **bridge**.

If all the teeth are missing or have to be taken out, the dentist replaces them with a full set of false teeth, or **denture**. First, impressions of the upper and lower jaws are taken and the false teeth are made from the impressions. The technician then sets the new teeth in wax, so that they can be moved around in the mouth until they fit properly. Next, they are set into natural-looking plastic.

Special tints are added so that the new teeth match the color of any remaining teeth. False teeth are made with great skill and look very natural these days.

▼ A dental technician works at his bench. Great care must be taken to make sure that dentures will fit the patient perfectly. Crowns are often made from porcelain, but dentures are usually plastic.

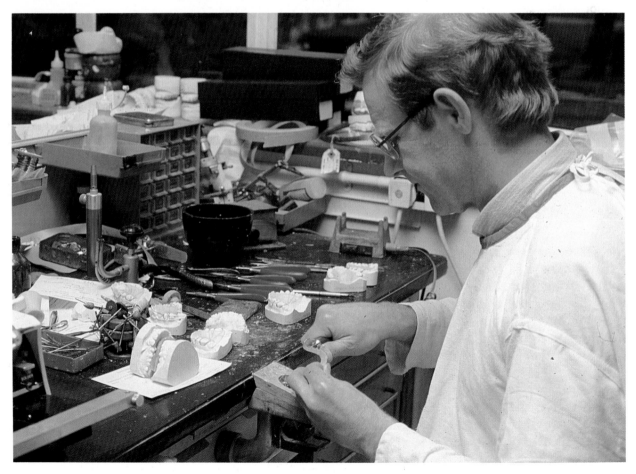

► This model shows how a bridge can be used to fix a false crown in position.

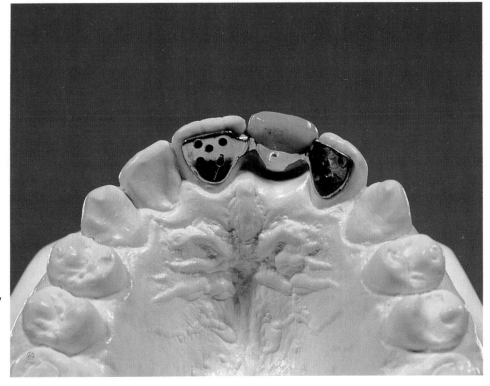

▼ When we are young, our teeth may grow crooked. An orthodontist can make braces which will straighten the teeth.

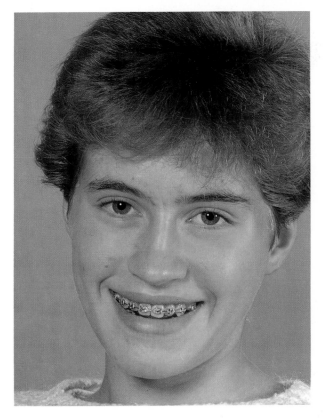

Looking Good

Some dental work is done to make your teeth look better. Sometimes, the jaw is too small and the teeth become crowded and crooked. If the teeth are overcrowded, it is difficult to clean them. This can lead to decay. Crooked teeth can lead to bad "bite." This means that the teeth do not meet properly when the jaw closes.

Orthodontia is the branch of dentistry which improves teeth by slowly moving them with springs and wires. This treatment may also help people to chew more easily because the teeth are lined up properly. Many people go to an orthodontist when they are in their early teens.

Impressions and X-rays are taken, and a great deal of planning is done before treatment starts. Sometimes, healthy teeth have to be removed to make more room. Then, a special **brace** made of metal and plastic will be fitted. This will gradually pull the teeth into the correct positions.

How We Look

The look of your skin, hair, and teeth can affect the way people think of you. You change the impression you make by changing your hairstyle and even by changing your teeth.

People have many reasons for changing their appearance. They may be going to a party, acting in a play, or going out for the day. Sometimes, people have scars or marks on their faces which they want to hide with makeup. They may have a hair color or style which they do not like.

Long Ago

People have tried to change how they look since the earliest times. In ancient Egypt, both men and women wore makeup. Many of the substances that have been used in makeup in the past are poisonous. The poison went in through the skin and the people often died. The Romans used to dye their hair. The dyes were so strong that their hair often fell out completely. Warriors painted and marked, or **tattooed**, their skin with complex patterns to frighten their enemies.

Wigs were worn both for beauty and to hide baldness. Two hundred years ago, the wigs became so large that mice sometimes lived in them as well as head lice and fleas!

Keeping Up Appearances

Many people still use makeup and alter the style and color of their hair. In the theater actors use makeup and wigs to change their appearances. In a circus, clowns use makeup to make their faces either funny or sad. In some countries, judges and lawyers wear wigs to show their position and authority.

◄ Painting on a clown's face can be fun! Clowns use makeup to change the appearance of their faces. A funny face can make us laugh. A sad face can make us feel sorry for the clown.

Young people often like to try new styles that may seem shocking to older people. They may have unique hair styles and dye their hair unusual colors. They may wear lots of makeup and even have tattoos. Sometimes, they will wear several earrings in one ear, or in both ears, or even in their noses.

A Natural Look

It can be fun to have a wild hairstyle and crazy makeup. However, too many strong hair dyes may damage the hair. Also, makeup must be cleaned off properly after every use or it may cause skin problems by blocking the pores.

Many people think that a natural look is nice. Whatever people may do to change their appearances, clean skin, shiny hair, and sparkling teeth always look good. They are a sign of good health.

▲ Boys in Thailand learn about the Buddhist religion by becoming monks for a short time. Their heads are shaved to mark the change in their lives.

▼ Teenage fashions often change from one extreme to another. These punks wear strange haircuts and makeup. Young people often enjoy looking very different.

Keeping Well-groomed

▼ In a traditional Japanese bathhouse, people soap and rinse themselves before plunging in. Then they can relax and chat with their friends.

The ways in which people keep their skin, nails, and hair in good condition vary in different parts of the world.

Soaping and Scrubbing

Early people kept their skin clean in much the same way as we wash and bathe ourselves today. The Gauls, a group of people who live in what is now France, made soap from wood ash and animal fat. The Romans built public baths wherever they went in Europe. Today, public baths are still popular in Japan. Some people bathe in mud, which they believe is good for their skin.

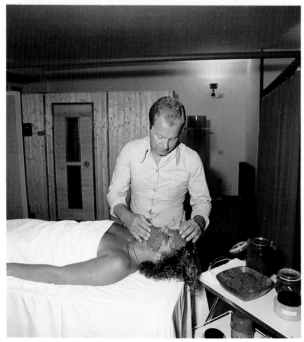

◄ Mineral-rich mud or health-giving herbs can be mixed up into a pack. This can be plastered on to the skin, and left to dry. When it is peeled off, the skin feels clean and healthy.

Steam Cleaning

Steam helps to clean the skin by making the body sweat. As the sweat runs down from the body, the dirt is washed away. Turkish baths, which use steam, have been popular for hundreds of years and are still found in many parts of the world. Native Americans used to have sweat tents or lodges. The sauna bath was invented in Finland, and it is now popular all over Europe and the United States.

In a sauna, hot steam is made by throwing water over heated stones. People sit in the steam for about fifteen minutes, and it makes them sweat and opens the pores in the skin. Then, they rub their bodies to loosen up the dirt. Finally, they jump into a bath of very cold water or take a cold shower. This rinses off the dirt and closes the pores in the skin. In some northern countries, the bathers run outside and roll in the snow!

Steam baths make people feel very clean and healthy, and they are a lot of fun.

However, sitting in hot, steamy baths is not always good for people who have any trouble with their breathing.

Skin, Hair, and Nails

Gentle rubbing, or massage, is good for the skin and the scalp. Massage helps to keep the skin in good condition and makes you relax.

Makeup and shampoos are often made from chemicals. Some newer kinds of makeup and some shampoos are made from natural things like plants. These are becoming very popular today. People are beginning to think that makeup containing chemicals may be harmful.

Along with caring for their skin and hair, some people have a manicure for their fingernails. During a manicure, the fingernails are shaped, cleaned, and polished. It is also possible to have the same things done to the toenails. This is called a pedicure. Most people simply keep their nails trimmed and scrubbed.

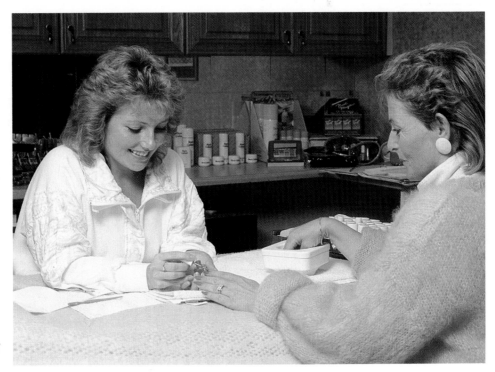

▶ A beautician paints a woman's nails. The nails have been filed and polished, so that they look elegant.

Accidents

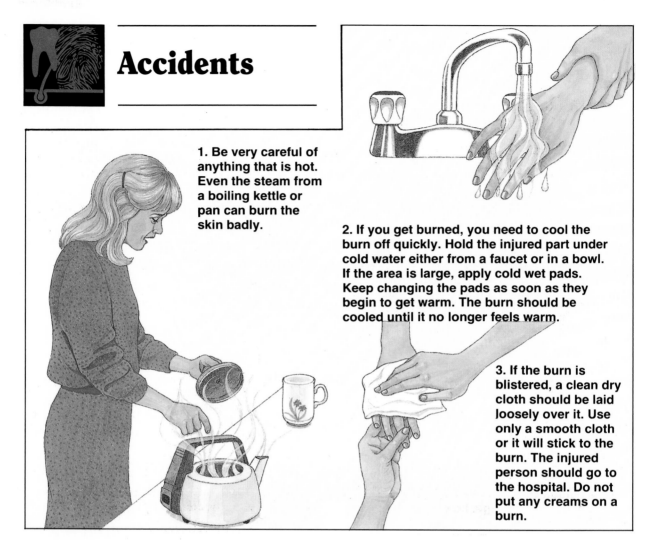

1. Be very careful of anything that is hot. Even the steam from a boiling kettle or pan can burn the skin badly.

2. If you get burned, you need to cool the burn off quickly. Hold the injured part under cold water either from a faucet or in a bowl. If the area is large, apply cold wet pads. Keep changing the pads as soon as they begin to get warm. The burn should be cooled until it no longer feels warm.

3. If the burn is blistered, a clean dry cloth should be laid loosely over it. Use only a smooth cloth or it will stick to the burn. The injured person should go to the hospital. Do not put any creams on a burn.

Accidents can happen even when you are at home or playing with your friends, so be careful.

If something does happen, do not panic! Call an adult right away. If you can, learn how to treat simple injuries with first aid. Then, you will know what to do until help arrives. The Red Cross, local police or fire departments, your school or youth groups may offer first aid courses.

Injured Skin

Large burns, wounds, and other injuries to the skin must be treated by a doctor. Small injuries can be dealt with by a person who knows first aid.

Even a small burn is painful, but running cold water over it will make it feel better. The cold water should be applied for at least ten minutes or until the burning feeling is gone.

Cover the burn with a clean, dry bandage. Never use anything made of fluffy material because it will stick to the wound. For the same reason, never put a sticky surface on a burn.

The victim of an animal bite should probably see a doctor, especially if the animal is wild or unfamiliar. The doctor might give the victim an injection to fight infection. The bite itself can be treated just like a small wound.

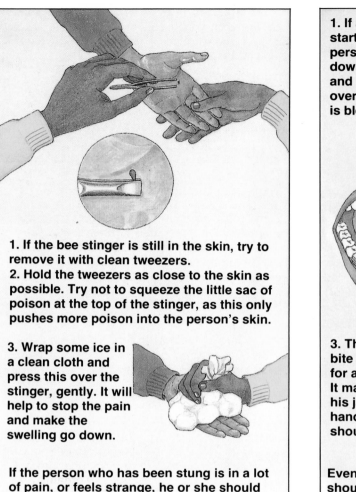

1. If the bee stinger is still in the skin, try to remove it with clean tweezers.
2. Hold the tweezers as close to the skin as possible. Try not to squeeze the little sac of poison at the top of the stinger, as this only pushes more poison into the person's skin.

3. Wrap some ice in a clean cloth and press this over the stinger, gently. It will help to stop the pain and make the swelling go down.

If the person who has been stung is in a lot of pain, or feels strange, he or she should see a doctor at once.

1. If a tooth socket starts to bleed, the person should sit down next to a table and lean his head over to the side that is bleeding.

2. Place a tightly folded, clean pad over the socket, but not in it. The top of the pad should be above the level of the teeth.

3. The person should bite hard on the pad for about 15 minutes. It may help if he rests his jaw in a cupped hand. The bleeding should stop.

Even if the bleeding does stop, the person should see a doctor or dentist as soon as possible.

When bees sting, the stinger must be removed from the skin. Wasp stings can often be treated with vinegar, lemon juice, or meat tenderizer.

A blister from rubbing or a burn should not be broken. If it is, it will become open to infection. A blister will usually go away on its own.

Toothache

Many accidents to teeth happen at swimming pools, or when playing a sport of any kind. Try and be especially careful. Do not run and fool around by the swimming pool where it is slippery underfoot.

If you damage a tooth, you will need to see a dentist as soon as possible. If a whole tooth is knocked out, it should be wrapped in a small pad soaked in a weak mixture of salt and water until you get to the dentist. A dentist can sometimes put the tooth back in place if you get to him or her quickly enough.

Sometimes, a tooth socket bleeds after a tooth has been knocked out. See a dentist as soon as you can.

You may be able to stop the bleeding by biting on a clean pad. Make sure that you tip your head to the side that is bleeding, so that the blood does not run into your throat.

Did You Know?

Skin Size
The skin of an adult person has an area of about two square yards, which is big enough to cover a twin bed. The whole skin of an adult weighs about fourteen pounds.

Fingerprints
The skin on each fingertip has little ridges in it. The ridges make up a pattern that you can see by inking a fingertip and pressing it onto a sheet of paper. Everyone has his or her own fingerprints. They are different from the fingerprints of everyone else in the world.

Sweating Buckets
There are about three million sweat glands in your skin. If you get very hot, your sweat glands can pour out as much as three quarts of sweat in an hour! You need to make up this loss of water, which is why you get very thirsty when it is hot, or after a lot of exercise.

▼ A microscope shows up the structure of the human skin. On this section of head skin, the epidermis has been colored red, and the dermis blue. The blood cells in the dermis have also been colored red. The larger, pinkish-white blobs are stores of fat, which help to keep us warm.

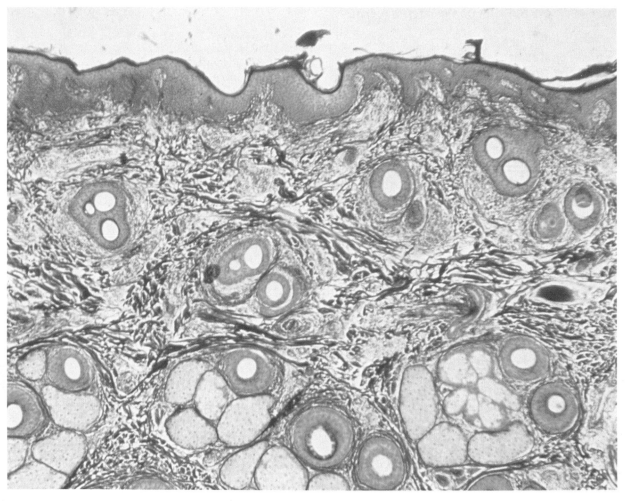

Hairy Monsters

The hairs on your head and in your eyebrows fall out after a while and new ones grow to replace them. Your eyebrow hairs last only three to five months, but head hairs last several years. If the hairs did not fall out, they would keep on growing. Your eyebrows would form two hairy curtains over your eyes and face. During your lifetime, if it did not fall out, the hair on your head could grow to a length of about twenty-six feet!

Hair and Nail Records

The longest growths of hair on record are twenty-six feet for head hair, seventeen and a quarter feet for a beard, and eight and a half feet for a mustache. The longest nail was a thumbnail which reached a length of thirty-four inches.

First Teeth

Only one person out of every 2,000 people is born with some teeth. Famous people who were born with teeth include Julius Caesar and Napoleon Bonaparte.

Touch Sensitive

You have thousands of nerves in your fingertips, which make them very sensitive to touch. You can feel two objects which are only 1/16 of an inch apart with your fingertips. However, on the skin of your thigh, the objects would have to be over three inches apart before you could tell that there were two of them. The center of your back has the fewest touch sensors.

▲ About 200 years ago, men and women wore wigs. Many became so large that mice were sometimes found nesting in them Cartoonists of the day loved to make fun of them.

► Murari Aditya has the world record for the longest fingernails. The nails of his left hand reached a total of 10 feet 2 inches in 25 years. They were cut off on a TV show in Japan in September 1986. Murari has started growing his nails again.

Glossary

acid: a strong, sour substance which can eat away solid things. Acids which attack teeth are made by bacteria.

acne: a skin infection common in teenagers. Pimples appear on the face, neck, and the top of the body.

albino: a person who has no coloring in the skin or hair. This makes the skin very pale and the hair white.

allergy: a sickness caused when something such as dust has an unusual effect on the body. Hay fever is caused by an allergy to pollen.

alopecia: a loss of hair, or baldness, in which patches of hair fall out.

amalgam: a mixture of metals that a dentist uses to fill a cavity in a tooth.

anesthetic: a substance that prevents people or animals from feeling pain.

antiseptic: a substance that kills germs. Liquids used for cleaning often have an antiseptic in them.

blackhead: a plug of oil that blocks one of the small holes in the skin. It has a dirty black top, which is why it is called a "blackhead."

blister: a watery or blood-filled swelling in the skin. Blisters are caused by severe pressure or burning.

boil: a painful swelling on the skin, caused by an infection.

brace: a set of wires worn in the mouth to straighten crooked teeth.

bridge: a false tooth that is kept in the mouth by being firmly attached to real teeth on either side.

calcium: a substance which we need for strong bones, teeth, and healthy muscles. Calcium is found in green, leafy vegetables and dairy foods.

cancer: a disease in which some of the cells of the body grow incorrectly and too quickly, and damage other cells.

canine: one of the four pointed teeth near the front of the mouth, used for tearing.

carotene: an orange-red coloring found in many plants and in humans. Carotene is changed to vitamin A by the body.

cell: a very small part or unit. Most living things are made up of millions of cells.

cementum: a thin bone-like material which covers the outside of the root of a tooth.

cortex: the outer layer of any part of the body, such as the brain, liver, or a hair.

crown: the top part of a tooth which shows above the gums. A false covering on a tooth is also called a crown.

cuticle: a layer of dead cells, especially the outer layer of a single hair or the skin around the base of a fingernail or toenail.

dandruff: small bits of skin that flake off from the skin on the head into the hair.

decay: material which has broken down. Tooth decay is caused by substances which eat through the hard outer layer of a tooth and create a cavity.

dentin: the yellow layer of a tooth beneath the very hard outer coating. Most of a tooth is made of dentin.

denture: a set of false teeth on a base. A denture is not attached to the mouth, and can be taken out for cleaning.

dermatitis: a skin problem. It makes the skin red and itchy or sore.

dermis: the layer of skin beneath the outside layer. "Dermis" means "skin" in Greek.

eczema: a skin problem that makes the skin red, often with crusting and flaking. The skin is usually very itchy.

enamel: the very hard surface of the tooth that contains calcium.

epidermis: the top layer of skin. The epidermis is the part you can see.

evaporation: changing from a liquid into a gas. Evaporation is caused by heat.

evolve: to change or develop slowly to become different. Living things will change to match their living conditions over long periods of time.

excavator: a power tool that the dentist uses to clean out the inside of a decayed tooth.

fibrin: a substance in blood which helps it to thicken, so that it will stop flowing out of a cut.

fluoride: a substance put in water or toothpaste that helps to prevent tooth decay.

follicle: a small channel in your skin from which a hair grows.

gene: a tiny part of each living cell. The gene controls how that cell is going to look or behave in a plant or animal

germ: a tiny living thing that can get into your body and cause disease. Germs include bacteria and viruses. Not all germs are harmful.

gland: a part of the body which makes a substance for the body to use. Different glands make different substances.

gum: the pink, firm flesh that surrounds the roots of our teeth.

head lice: small creatures that can live in hair. They irritate the skin and cause health problems.

hormone: a substance made in the body to trigger changes like growth. Hormones are carried around the body in the blood.

impression: an imprint of a hard object made in something soft. Impressions of teeth and the shape of the jaw are made in wax or plaster. The molds made from these are used to make dentures, or braces.

incisor: one of the sharp, square teeth at the front of the mouth. It is used for cutting. There are four incisors in each jaw.

infectious disease: an illness which can be caught from other people or animals. The germs that cause infectious diseases often grow in water or in dirty places.

injection: a way of putting medicine very quickly into the body through a needle pushed straight into the bloodstream. A doctor or dentist may give an injection to stop pain.

keratin: the tough substance in your hair and nails. The surface of your skin is also covered with keratin.

medulla: the central area of a part of the body such as a single hair.

melanin: a black or dark brown coloring found in the skin and hair.

microscope: an instrument which makes very small objects look much larger. With it, you can see things that are too small for your eyes to see alone.

milk teeth: the first set of teeth that a child grows.

mineral: a non-living substance that the body needs in small amounts to stay healthy.

molar: a tooth at the back of the mouth that is used for crushing and grinding.

muscle: a type of material in the body which can shorten itself to produce movement.

nerves: part of a network of tiny "cables" which pass messages from all parts of the body to the brain and back again.

ointment: medicine mixed with an oil or grease, so that it can be put on the skin.

orthodontia: the treatment of teeth to make them grow straight and even. The person who gives this treatment is called an orthodontist.

parasite: a tiny creature that lives on another animal or human body. Parasites take food from the body and often cause disease.

pigment: a substance in plants or animals that gives color. It is found in leaves, fur, hair, or skin.

plaque: a sticky film that grows on your teeth, and causes decay.

pore: a tiny hole in your skin. Sweat comes out of pores. Blocked pores cause pimples.

premolar: a tooth near the back of the mouth. It is used for grinding food.

probe: a tool used by a dentist to get bits of food out of the teeth. It is also used to find cavities that need filling in the teeth.

puberty: the age when a child's body changes and becomes an adult body.

pulp: the soft center of a tooth.

quick: any area of skin that feels pain or touch very easily, especially underneath a nail.

rash: a skin problem in which small red marks cover the skin. A rash may itch.

ringworm: a disease in which there are ring-shaped itchy patches on the skin. Hair may fall out in clumps also.

scalp: the skin that covers the top of the head under the hair.

scar: a mark left on the skin after a deep wound heals.

sebaceous glands: small glands in the under layer of the skin that make protective oil.

sebum: a kind of oil that covers and protects your skin and hair and is made by the sebaceous glands.

sensitive: describes something which reacts quickly to touch or pain.

shaft: a long narrow tube or pole.

skin graft: a way of treating burns and bad wounds by taking skin from another part of the body to cover the damaged area.

subcutaneous tissue: a layer of fat just beneath your skin. Subcutaneous tissue is thicker in some parts of the body than in others.

sweat: a watery fluid containing some body wastes and salt which passes out of the body through the skin. Sweating helps to keep the body cool.

tattoo: marks that people make to decorate their skin. The marks are made by piercing the skin with a needle and putting in dye.

temperature: a measure of heat. Human body temperature is normally about 98.6°F.

ultraviolet: invisible rays that come from the sun. We need these rays to stay healthy, but too much of them is harmful.

white blood cells: special cells in the blood that fight disease.

X-rays: invisible rays that pass through solid objects. X-ray photographs show the inside of the body or teeth.

Index